4TH GRADE HISTORY: ANCIENT CIVILIZATIONS

SPEEDY PUBLISHING

Speedy Publishing LLC
40 E. Main St. #1156
Newark, DE 19711
www.speedypublishing.com

Ancient civilization refers specifically to the first settled and stable communities that became the basis for later states and nations.

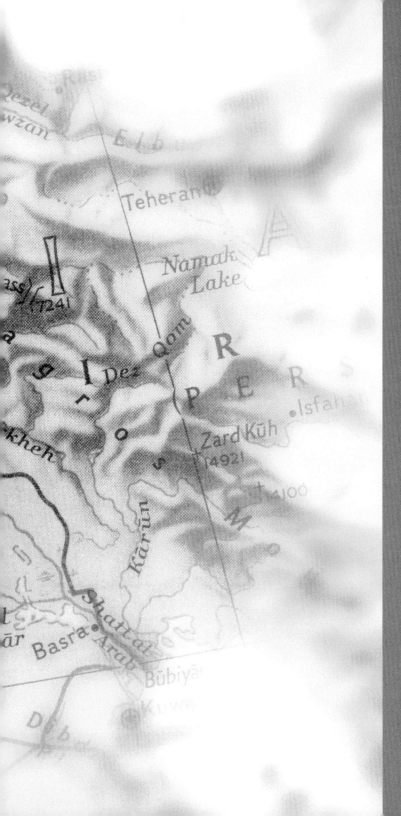

Mesopotamia is widely considered to be the cradle of human civilization. It was here that people first gathered in large cities, learned to write, and created governments.

The Indus Valley Civilization was one of three early civilisations of the Old World, and the most widespread among them. The Indus Civilization may have had a population of more than 5 million.

Ancient Egypt was a civilization of ancient Northeastern Africa. The ancient Egyptians are known for their astonishing culture, the ever standing pyramids and the sphinx.

The ancient Mayan civilization thrived in Central America from about 2600 BC. The ancient Mayans were brilliant astronomers and mathematicians.

Ancient Greece was one of the most influential civilizations. Ancient Greece produced many magnificent achievements in areas of government, science, philosophy and the arts that still influence our lives.

Ancient Rome began on the Italian Peninsula as early as the 8th century BC. Rome became one of the largest empires in the ancient world.

Andean civilizations are mainly based on the cultures of Ancient Peru. The Inca Empire was the last sovereign political entity that emerged from the Andean civilizations.